# STICKS AND STONES AND SMALL FISH BONES

# STICKS AND STONES AND SMALL FISH BONES

Winston Earle

YMWC

Karen Parris has been my friend for over forty years. We grew up together as literal neighbors. She lived in the house next to me. Through the years we have supported each other from afar through loves gained and lost, turmoil and joys in life, emotionally and spiritually by just being there for each other. Karen is an artist in her own right and, in her medium, far better and more talented than I in mine. It is because of her that I came up with the title for this collection and some of the poetry within. This book would not exist without her love and support.

Front cover image was created using CoPilot AI
Back cover image was created using CoPilot AI

# TABLE OF CONTENTS

# 1 00 WAYS

One hundred pages means one hundred ways to spill the ink.
Still one hundred stays.
To challenge skills in rhyme and wordplay
and other styles to have prose sway
the hearts and minds of those who choose to read:
listen when the prose is vocally freed
to spread the hidden in each word's seed,
destined to grow to meet its potential's need.
One hundred pages to change the old.
Reveal some truths with love that's bold.
To warm the blood when the weather's cold
and make one think. Despite what we're told.
One hundred ways to spill the ink.
One hundred avenues down which to think.
One hundred thousand misses if you blink,
but only fifty thousand if you wink.
One hundred stays, despite the words.
Despite the myriad sounds you've heard.
As varied as insects, fish, and birds.
One hundred stays. It's not demurred.
One hundred pages wait for me,
demanding my pen sets them free.
For my ink is their company
when their creations we can see.

## MOMENT

Let's talk about the moment.
Right here. Right now.
Let's scream at the top of our lungs
about the opportunity this moment brings.
Presently. Currently. Now.
We can slip into the existence
of the world as we've dreamed it.
We can take the first step into utopia.
The moment- this moment-
is where we can be what we want to see.
Now. Right now. We can do what we believe is true.
In this present, we can create our fate.
All we need to do is act on instinct;
on necessity; on our dreams and true desires.
We get to know ourselves wholly.
Live our lives truly.
Create our truths wisely.
To see our dreams clearly.
Once this moment is gone-
here's the great part:
If we are conscious, truthful and committed,
we get to do it all again without doubt.
In the next moment.

## NIGHTMARE LOVE

Love in the sunshine. Love in the rain.
Loving is loving, until loving is pain.
Love can make us angry. Love can make us sad.
Love can be the best thing and the worst we've ever had.
It's better to have loved and lost than never have loved at all.
Stated by a lover, whose love has yet to fall.
Love can take us higher than the stars we see at night:
Yet drag us, yelling and growling through every lover's fight.
When we can forgive our dears, we learn to rise above.
When we can forgive ourselves, well, that's when we know love.
Love accepts the faults and foibles and their mistakes too.
Even the egregious when that love is true.
Although, love sometimes brings pain, it sometimes can be said,
those times when we are all alone, it's lack of love we dread.
Love can bring the moon out, when life seems to be dark.
In darkness, figurative or not, love ignites a spark.
There're songs of love, plays of love, and anecdotes for years.
We live for love and die for love and miss it through our tears.
We want to die when love deserts us; hide like cats from the rain.
Yet, the next chance we have for love, we do it all again.
So, take your love and spread it wide.
Help someone's life turn bright.
So, no one has to suffer through another loveless night.

## ONCE BITTEN

Some call the beast a monster
because it stalks us every day.
Some call the beast a fact of life.
Face it and accept its way.
Some say it's not a beast at all,
for from it you cannot run.
Stare in its eyes and try your best
and you can still have your fun.
Please know that the beast will bite you.
Its venom reacts really slow.
At first, it won't seem to affect you,
but as time moves on, you'll know.
You'll feel yourself getting weaker,
although your muscles might not shrink.
You'll begin moving slower.
No longer as quick as you think.
On thinking, things start to get foggy.
Things easily known start to fade.
Still, time may seem to move faster,
though longer the plans that you've made.
Longer, until heal, your injuries.
Fast healing days will be no more.
You can no longer afford to be careless,
as pain rises from injuries before.
Some people seem much, much older.
What was youthful has come and gone.
The venom sometimes drains their vitality
so everything about them seems wrong.
Some do everything to keep the beast tame
and locked in its very own cage.
This beast no cage can hold, and its bite has no cure,
for this beast has one name:

It's age.

NEW RULES
Look how low the mighty have fallen.
So low that the mighty are mighty no more.
The giants are down, and the titans are crawling.
Their former heights are memories they bore.
There was a time we all were eschewing.
the roads upon which the mighty would move.
Yet those same roads would become their undoing;
their weakness; their torture; their uneven groove.
It's crazy how much the mighty have taken:
our dignity, freedom, riches and too...
their levies on just about all we were making.
Our children. Our crops. Our toys. Even our shoes.
But now they're diminished, and we are the titans
imbued with the potion of changing the rules:
And we will! With focus on dictums that heightens,
and leaves not one of us acting like fools.
The formerly mighty have taught us the motions
that lead to oppression, discord, and hate.
Our new rules will create satisfaction,
so, every last one of us avoids the same fate.

## DREAMS OF

Ah. There it is. The fire that's burning up my heart.
Is it just the earth's desire tearing me apart?
When I was a little boy, I would begin to cry.
Now I just get angry. I wish the world would fry.
Still, I know there's processes; small steps we get to take.
Though I can see desired goals we'll achieve when we awake.
Cancel the current nightmares. Redefine our needs.
Prioritize the love inside to make the rules we heed.
Absquatulate the victim's fear to substitute with truth
revealed by our creator so none of us need proof.
Then all of us so filled with love can share it with a smile.
Without a single thought of fear, untruths, or death, or guile.
At night when pillows touch our heads,
we'll sleep and dream of love.
No anger, sadness, pain or doubt, just freedom to dream of.

## VOCAL REMINISCENCE

Thunder from the mouths of babes crying for the teat,
until they've teeth strong enough for solid food and meat.
They'll be indoctrinated, the majority as slaves,
by common institutions that instruct how to behave.
The world will steal their thunder, and they'll whimper instead.
Impotence their trademark; fear injected in their head.
Then, they will fall to darkness and forget they were the light,
believing they must be restrained, they not knowing what's right.
That thunder was their calling- the truth they knew while young.
The confidence to call out all that God had done.
A vocal reminiscence of a power that's divine
until irradiated by beliefs of man and time.
To have a strong society, of course we must behave.
Yet, that doesn't translate into owner over slave.
God exists in all of us and everything we see.
Although we think we can, we can't, escape divinity.
We're each afforded choice, to exercise free will.
So, we can grow a better world or just keep it ill.
But given that we have a choice, one must stop and wonder,
why we'd ever choose to surrender our God-given thunder.

## UNBURDENED CREATIVITY

I keep my creativity trapped inside a gilded box,
and listen to the noise as it fights the iron locks.
It pains my beating heart to limit myself so,
but this way my hidden talents I don't have to show.
I know my creativity is longing to be free.
If I let a little out, it will reveal all of me.
My friends and family tell me that what they've seen is good.
If they knew they were capable, they'd show it if they could.
Still, they don't know the secret; the pain I'm trying to hide.
I feel I have the wrath of man hidden deep inside.
Maybe, I enjoy it and my creativity
would release a love of chaos for the world to see.
See, I know that from nothing there's just possibility
and that in each moment we create reality.
I think that I'm afraid of what I might create.
Or maybe I'm afraid that I might just be great.
Or I'm afraid of ridicule from my family and friends.
Or I'll reveal reality- how far from it we bend.
As I pause to ponder what changes I could make,
I realize I've locked away the only thing to slake
my wrath, my pain, my sadness; and release my joy.
I see how I cheat myself each time fear I employ.
I produce the golden key that opens iron locks;
release my creativity I had trapped inside a box.
I release all the tension I've held onto for a while
as unburdened creativity helps to make me smile.

## STICKS AND STONES

Sticks and stones and small fish bones
were used to stunt our growth.
Thanks to the use of sticks and tricks,
all they got was close.
Sticks were swung and bells were rung,
but minds were never trapped.
Winds from the missed tinged pains of hits;
from experience we're rapt.
Stones were thrown to break our bones.
Experience and speed prevailed.
We stayed low. Got in the flow.
Over our heads they sailed.
Then they tried to blind us;
deprive us of the truth.
Hide our very origins
so history has no proof.
Loyal words taint things we've heard;
limit our verbal breadth.
Small fish bones choke true words spake,
to lead us to our death.
Still, words are harmless by themselves
until meanings are applied.
Confused by every statement made,
we realize they've lied.
Now we stand unconscious
and confused with what we know
about what creation is hiding
and where we're supposed to go.
Sticks and stones and small fish bones
may take my breath away.
Experience, books, and measured looks
will teach me how to stay.

## GROWN

Grown!

Walking up steps of a life that's owned.

Making sure our hearts and legs are toned.

Hoping we don't walk this life alone.

We're grown.

Fighting off demons that want our souls.

Learning all we need to reach our goals.

Accepting only things that keep us whole.

That's grown.

Experience used to make us smart.

Happiness shining from our hearts.

Knowing that love is where it starts.

Owning our rights and wrongs are part

of everything combined that makes us... grown.

Grown out.

Grown through.

Grown in.

Grown.

## BLUEBIRD

I enjoyed the new life of spring's reverie,
until the spring bluebird set its eyes on me.
Then, all I could see of my future path
was the season to come:
humidity, heat and summer's wrath.
I decided to do like my old leather shoes
and walk a mile through the spring bluebird's blues.
Where the heat would oppress and the thunderstorms tease,
lightning sets fire fueled by warm summer's breeze.
Let's flip the coin to the more joyous side.
Kids are noisy and loud as they're playful and wild.
The bluebird's now flown to a much cooler place,
while I go on living in this much hotter space
and forget that I see the bluebird no more.
As I try to stay cool, I head for the shore.
But wait! It's still spring. I prognosticate heat.
The breezes are mild. The weather, a treat.
The bluebirds are grazing and fluttering around,
increasing their strength for the places they're bound.
I can enjoy spring right here and the breeze right now
despising summer's heat when spring takes its bow.

## NIGHT'S LIGHT

Well, at first there was only Night.
Then, Day stepped in to play.
The time between them had to be shared.
So, half Night's time went away.
Day began creating;
from firmament to ground.
Everything on one flat plain,
but Night said: "make them round".
"Separate them into groups.
I'll hold them in my space.
Light them all as you see fit.
I'll keep them in my place.
I'll spin them on an axis
so they can stay afloat,
so new things you can practice-
to them your time devote."
But Night then reacted:
"I must make them lean.
Thus, sometimes you'll be exalted
and sometimes you'll be demeaned.
There're times they'll gather all your light.
They'll dance and sing and play.
There're other times my dark will bite;
inside they'll mostly stay.
Your light will bring them warmth and growth,
my dark, a winter's chill.
Life will thrive and grow in both,
but with dark this requires will."
Day stared at Night and Night at Day.
Day smiled a wicked grin.
Night wondered just what Day's play was.
Day asked: "They have to spin?"

Night nodded the affirmative:
"If not, they'll fall apart"
Day's smile grew much more positive:
"I've ideas I want to start."
Night's eyes squinted sharply,
as Day cleared its throat:
"This presentation's hardly
 in a state to promote.
I'd have surprised you later, Night.
You brought it up too soon.
To light your space, I created this orb.
I think I'll call it moon."

## THE REALM

We live in the realm of the stolen,
believing the words, "we are free".
Where things we produce have more value,
and our value is less than money.
The wealthy have become our new gods,
whose Olympus we can't even find.
Our leaders bend knee to their power,
while the people are losing their minds.
The land once belonged to the natives,
but they were wiped out by a plague.
The realm was developed by what schools call great men.
The history of that is now vague.
In its start, the realm had great cultures;
values mixed like stew in a pot.
Now the realm is divided between
those who claim to have and have not.
Looking at the party that has not,
divided again group by group.
Influenced by their own minor gods
to fight for respect to recoup.
Even amongst the new gods,
status is measured by scale.
It's not just the money that's valued.
It's the power to alter detail.
Here in the realm of the stolen,
the gods, nor the masses, are safe.
They all sacrifice centuries old lessons
in a world that seeks them to replace.
Their defenders have become diminished.
Their culture also lost its way.
Their options are rapidly fading,
decreasing with each passing day.

The realm of the stolen will transform.
"You're free" will be much less than words.
Uttered by desperate people
who just wish for their words to be heard.


UNBRIDLED
Sometimes we rise above our circumstance.
We exercise our power within:
Interpreting our challenges
as opportunities for massive growth.
In those blessed moments,
we direct love to ourselves
by living in our highest state
and creating the joy we want to see.
During those times, all that shows
is the inner light of possibility
realized as potential unbridled.

## PILLARS

I noted the rusty pillars
of a life abused by sin
and thought of the cold dark corners
that for me existed within.
I dropped to my knees and mumbled
a prayer that no one else heard.
I asked for a little mercy
as to God I did give my word.
My word to live life more peacefully.
My word to live life with love.
My word to in life be giving.
My word like Christ up above.
My word to lift others with me
despite the fear I may feel.
To provide the steps to right living
and the power acts of love reveal.
"Your words," a higher voice told me,
"commits you to what you just said.
The actions you next take before me
decides how your life will be read."
Rising to my full standing stature,
I stepped from the place where I'd knelt.
I confidently strode towards my future
with power from those words I'd felt.
Now I look at these pillars
and see sparkling metal beneath.
The rust falls away, like dark orange plaque,
the metal's like shiny white teeth.

## ALL WE GOT

Sometimes someone else's words drive the pen.

Sometimes all we got is the ink.

Sometimes words initiated in the mind

fail to make it to the throat, the tongue, the hand, the quill.

Faith is believing in the unseen.

The unknowable. The untouchable.

Sometimes that fails too.

Sometimes someone else's words are all we got-

to rebuild belief.

To remind us we're great.

To reveal our strength.

To renew our faith.

In our God.

In our love.

In ourselves.

Once those else words touch our ears,

open our minds, close our eyes, ignite our knowing,

then our pen can write our heart,

expose our soul

so, all can see, can hear, can know-

All we got.

## FIVE DECADES OF TENUOUS SMILES

Forward movement slowed? So what?

Creation drives this train.

Seeing that, knowing that,

"Why?" rises more and more.

"Why not?" answer without resistance.

Movement continues forward.

Reminiscence peaks behind, smiling at days

long dulled by "Now",

yet brightened by memories' longing.

The lessons from the darker past

seem quaint now, with gratitude's forgiveness.

Eyes close. Cool breezes wash my face.

Life brought me to today.

Creation pushes me as five decades of tenuous smiles

guides each step forward.

More relaxed and sure, with gifts to use and thoughts to share,

my contribution to a better world is assured.

Like creation, I'll move on to newer things before me.

HIDDEN
Is it a sin to be tired of living,
when there's not much for which one does care?
Or is there indifference to the thought of winning,
with little towards which one dares?
I've seen the sun rise and set on oceans:
Indian, Atlantic, Pacific too.
I've stepped foot on lands still and in motion;
on places at war, and conflicts few.
I've walked across paradise, seen hidden terrors.
Slept in the cold on rocky steeps.
Survived explosions of ballistic errors.
Seen creatures that walk, crawl, and creep.
I've flown over mountains
and swam under seas.
Seen people just break down
- fall to their knees.
Worked where the wind blows,
and my canteens freeze.
Saw only the milky way
could have stars like these.
Perhaps that's why I should continue my path
 to experience what God has created.
Let that be my joy and let go of my wrath
and all the things in life that I've hated.
There are people I love and those that love me
that I would not want left behind.
No matter the law, I know I am free
to be giving and gentle and kind.
Let's not forget change and its constant surprises
that sometimes leaves people morose.
But just like fresh rain there'll be new sunrises
and a hidden smile if we look close.

## TIME SPACE

Have you heard? The future is coming.
Tell me... Have you heard?
It's approaching with the speed of time.
At least that's what I've heard.
"It will never get here,"
a wise man said to me.
"Right now, was yesterday's future.
At least that much you must see.
Thus, the future cannot get here,
if here, now, we are to be."
Tell me... have you heard?
Have you heard?
The present is here and passing,
Not to be held in place.
Something the physicists tell me
is tied to time and space.
Have you heard? Have you heard? Have you heard?
The past cannot be changed.
Our memories may distort it.
Sometimes its truth seems strange.
Heard or not, don't matter.
It's time I can't exchange.

## AN EVENT OBSERVED BY TIME

Time watches us make fools of ourselves.
trying to extend its standing.
It watches change, constant in its presence,
as we try to move backwards in its space,
remembering falsely the realities of yesterday.
Still, time is measured in events passing
counted to contort its movement forward.
Combined with space, some see its stability
warped by the gravity of massive things
while stretching to the edges of the heavens-
A firmament carrying us onward even as space stretching,
is observed by time.
We will become extinct halfway through its blink
without being missed by time.
Surrendering our space to what comes next...
An event observed by time.

## A CERTAIN TRADE

We missed a certain trade-
of love, of gifts, of ideas-
sailing on to something different.
A stretch. A challenge. A hope for a fantasy fulfilled,
only to be left with the ashes of a duo compromised by deceits.
Fueled by traditions and what is "supposed" to be,
we sit alone on a pedestal, watching others do the same.
Comfortable in our habits. Challenged by our choices.
Sallying forth to take on the world
while emotional partnership calls,
knocks at our doors and slides down the flaw greased ladders
 of our self-assigned glory.
We are happy and alone.
Worthy and resistant.
At peace with our solo journey while in search of the companion
that will accept our flow.
We might be good for each other,
but simply wave from our perches.
We miss a certain trade of emotions. Of gifts. Of ideas.
Sailing past one challenge- to satisfy a need.

## WORDS FROM OUR MOUTH

The words from our mouth, the things that we said,
can be very different from what goes on in our head.
The need to be right, the fight to be sure,
encourages the search for our words to be pure.
Do our words match our feelings? Are our feelings on point?
Are our actions in concert with the words we anoint?
Do we do what we say? Do we say what we mean?
Though the point may be dirty, are the words we say clean?
Are intentions made known? Do our actions define
what our words indicate direct or sublime?
Reliability and fortitude; are they shown to be true?
Or simply words from our mouths. Do we say what we do?
It's the actions that count, sometimes words that we say,
that confirms that we're serious and not out to play.
If our actions at night match our words in the light
words from our mouth might represent and be right.
If the words that we say defy actions we mean,
the task in our life becomes ourselves to redeem.

## SLIGHTLY TWISTED REMIX

Clear days, in many ways,
signal our path to opportunity.
Removing the first obstacle to movement,
we are given sunshine and warmth.
Everything else is up to us.
We get to take first steps
and push for seconds and thirds.
Stepping towards the future
with lessons from our past.
Creating a path we desire
through intention and grit.
Ending with new beginnings
and open possibilities:
a slightly twisted remix
from what our fears expected.

## WORKDAYS

It's the first Monday of the week.
It'll be a great day, although the sky looks bleak.
There's not a single Monday that was made for the meek,
but this is where we start the search for wealth that we seek.
Tuesday is filled with its own surprise.
The second Monday that we must rise,
to execute the plans that we devise
so, what we complete can grow in size.
Wednesday's hump day, so we say.
Two more days then we can play.
We'll get started, with no delay,
to put our great work on display
Thursday's here! A day to seize.
As you well know, it's Friday eve.
You think, slow down, don't be naïve.
Tomorrow's end leaves you relieved.
Friday! Yes! The weekend's here!
The day that makes you want to cheer.
The next two days just can't compare.
To the joy that Fridays seem to share.

## THE CONDITION

High praise for the human condition.
Yes... and let's damn it just the same.
Born from love, anger, or pain
with curiosity and innocence to guide it.
We are nurtured with that love, that anger, that pain.
Add fear, dysfunction, compunction and hunger.
Deep inside, sometimes in the bowels of our souls,
we want connection.
We suffer the desires of a soul seeking to adjoin
with the source of its creation:
That creation by which it is surrounded.
Still, in circles drawn to the attraction of its creations,
we strive to scream- "Look at me!... For I am creator
and control what I have done!"-
while that voice, that quiet, whispering, loving voice,
speaks from a light in the soul that calls it back home.
The path to which we constantly stride,
judging crossroad after crossroad with each step,
until, as far as we know, the crossroads end
and we face consequences for each choice.
Damnation or salvation, we fear the coming end.
We want to extend our contribution to the human condition.
Outlive our competition by life, deed, or tribute
despite the wealth of our experience,
the truth of our existence,
or the journey towards our enlightenment
that the human condition motivates.
We exist on a train to a brighter way:
A conveyance back to creation while never having left it.
We are what we think, say, and do.
Good or bad. Works or fails. Better or worse.
Our actions can color our being; our existence.

Change can hasten our enlightenment.
Enlightenment can have us conscious as creators within creation.
The human condition is creation's condition.
Incubation for embryos. Waiting to emerge.

## NAÏVE ANGEL

I am a naïve angel
that sees the best in man.
Aware of their potential
beyond their current stance.
I see their souls awakening
despite their love of things.
When they prioritize each other
that's when they'll get their wings.
Right now, they fight for power,
displayed by what they've got.
Their title, job, or status,
but power these are not.
They tear each other down
like life exists through hate.
While most religions speak of love
that practice isn't great.
Deceive, discredit, destabilize;
destroy they don't say but they do.
Prioritized desire
they no longer know what's true.
The commitment to greatness
that's received positively,
is often skewed by fear and doubt
 and viewed so cautiously.
The pristine soul at each man's birth
is scarred by many flaws,
and those we seek to rectify
creating tainted laws.
They recognize their fumbles;
deny you should have yours.
Lover of many- self-proclaimed-
while you're labeled a whore.

Many speak of helping hands
with words that do sound sweet,
ensuring that their action
blocks the road that rubber meets.
To lift their names, they gladly sing
their praises to their Gods.
Meanwhile, they neither spare the child
nor spoil the future rods.
Man has focused on itself
as separate from it all.
So, now the unseen tie-ins
will precipitate their fall.
The world they took advantage of
accelerates its path.
The future that they can't predict
enshrined inside their math.
The floods, the storms, the earthquakes,
the sliding poles and more.
Their hubris does account for them
though the process came before.
Thus, as a naïve angel
that sees the best in man,
aware of their potential
I do believe they can.
Entrust their hearts to others
while lifting high their souls.
Work in love together
while achieving all their goals.
Place neighbors before dollars
and things we can replace.
Accept that there's more value
in their hearts, their souls, their face.
Stop judging by skin color,
or culture, or birthplace.

Recognize together
is the way to win this race.
You've got to see the God in you
is the same in someone else
That there but for the grace of God,
could have gone yourself
Raise your youth to survive alone
and as part of the world's stage
So that they may grow up
to create a better age
 Know that your potential
exceeds what you can see
 I am a naïve angel,
so I just let you be.

## THE BLACK MAN

I am a black man!
My body may be lithe and strong, but I am greater than its fibers
Even as slave I am master of my fate
I am a black man
My name is spirit, for first, that is what I am
Rising to my highest self
Being more than man makes me
I am a black man
My consort is the black woman
Who holds me beyond what I can see
Who loves me passionately beyond deserving
Then raises me, holds me, praises me
Though she is greater than me... or because of it
I am the black man
Aware of truths untold and things unseen
Fierce even with hands tied
Free though shackled and bound
Wise beyond the telling of our story
I am the black man
As a baby I'm breathing
As a toddler I'm needing
As a child I'm learning
As a teen I'm rebelling
As a young adult I'm capable
In midlife just grateful
As an elder, a teacher
I am the black man
Almost extinct
So they want us to think
Because we're the first link
Still, we rise from the brink
I am the black man

We fight for our sons
Overcoming our cultured ignorance
Uplifting our daughters to their natural greatness
Recognize our power in our will
Our knowledge in our talents
Our love in our hearts
And our creation in our souls
I am the black man
We share without giving
Grow without knowing
Love without touching
Live without being
I am the black man
Happiness finds us
Laughter soothes us
Love binds us
Hatred chains us to the greatness of our spirit
 And the gratitude that we are here
With what we've got... Together

MAD DASHES

I stand on the pinnacle of my life's being- now.
Aware of the wonder of my eyes seeing- how.
The world that I'm a part of- believing I'm not,
that I guess I helped create. Yeah, that's all I've got.
For my inaction was action still- that's right! I watched.
A voyeur to each day's events- for fear action I'd botch.
I lived with the fears- conjured in my mind.
But sometimes I'd act- with courage I would find.
I'd change someone's life- and sometimes my own.
Watch them find success- feel pride down to my bones.
So now I can see the fear- my mind made.
How it's overcome-with courage in trade.
Now here I stand on top of my game.
Seeing that fear is how only in name.
I step down the slope- knowing I can
- to defeat my fears as a brave man.

## THE TEST

Climbing higher mountains,
like living higher lives,
answers many questions and doubts.
Making newer trails,
facing older fears,
helps with understanding what life is about.
Knowing this
and doing this
are two completely different things.
Walking on the ground
thinking you can fly
won't necessarily help you spread your wings.
But when you start to look at life
as terminal at best,
you can sit and let it pass
or step up and take the test.

INSANE

Flavors fall from the sky in drops.
Inspiring words that describe
why I'm here poetically, rhetorically,
intentionally, creatively but not factually.
My mind seems to grasp the concepts
as pictures of facts that could be,
but remain unable to describe these sights
in words.
Thus, truths that might set all souls free
are trapped in my head, remaining mystery,
while the words I utter in explanation
make me sound insane
and the world keeps turning around.

## JUST GIVE IT ONE MORE DAY (ANTHEM)

Born at least twelve years ago, this one's almost a teen.
With friends of almost equal age, some lovely, some quite mean.
The lovely make you happy. With them you love to play.
The mean, they make things ugly. Just give it one more day.
The mean, you think, have power to make your life a mess.
The truth is they have nothing. We're all equally blessed.
The mean are really just as scared, no matter what they say.
The truth will come into the light. Just give it one more day.
Sometimes we feel like failures. Seems like nothing will go right.
No matter how hard we try, we're stuck in this dark plight.
The truth is it's our viewpoint; our actions… words we say.
View things as a lesson learned. Just give it one more day.
The dark days that may slow us, they're challenges at worst.
The things that make us better so we can come in first.
For each and every moment, however it displays,
Is meant to teach us something. Just give it one more day.
We're put on Earth to learn things to brighten heart and soul.
Enlightenment and loving are, deep inside, our goal.
So, love yourself and someone else. See love; be love today.
And that love will return to you. Just give it one more day.

BLAZED

I sat and smoked the day away
Caught in the confusion of my own creation
Lost as I was in a myriad of objectives
Without a single plan in sight
I took to vice to calm my nerves
Attempting to clear my head of distress
But I became more aware of
What I had to do and what needed to be done
The stress increased and I had to move
The bud bounced as it hit the ground
Ash blazed everywhere
Only to gray as it cooled
Stomping it out as I rose
I began my journey to accomplishment
And blazed across my life
A shooting star from that point to the end

## A SINGLE STEP

They said "a single step" was all it took. That didn't work for me.
Several steps I've taken, and still nothing I see.
Did I do it wrong? Start on the wrong foot?
Or could it have been the wrong path I took?
Was there some obstacle that got in the way?
Without knowing where I'm going, it's so hard to say.
I'm seeking help now from the masters of this.
To correct my path so I don't remain pissed.
She told me the journey is long and it is hard.
I'll end up physically, emotionally, and mentally scarred.
"A single step" he said, "and the journey begins.
Sometimes you will lose big time and sometimes you will win.
Be grateful for the present and where you stand right now.
You can't see the end and you won't know how.
A single step commenced the journey to the future you see,
but right now, you're where you're supposed to be".

## THE FREEDOM

Love the freedom. Love the choice.
Love the chance to use my voice.
Love the opportunity to shout:
"LOOK AT ME! SEE ME! I'M FREE!"
Now's the time to take the chance
to rise up high, then sing and dance.
To flow across this continent;
go everywhere that Jesus went.
To spread the word of love and faith.
To man. To woman, teen and waif.
To create in society
a culture based on unity.
Love the freedom. Love the chance
to share this love with all perchance,
to show the world while we are free,
still, there's accountability.
First for self and what we do
and to our higher selves be true.
Then to others as they rise to help them,
as they reach their prize.
To let others be who they are
though we find it strange, sometimes bizarre.
Forgiving those who harm us still;
they may be slow; they may be ill.
Love freedom's variety.
The amazing things we get to see
The fantastic things we get to learn.
The opportunities at every turn.
Love the power of each word that's uttered
in the truths you've heard.
That's twisted to bend reality
and hide the fact that we are free.

Words uttered to make us laugh.
Words whispered to change our path.
Words sung sweetly to calm our nerves.
Words from those unknown we serve.
Each word can hold a mystery
and change our very history.
So, love the freedom Love the facts.
In every moment we can act.
Knowing that freedom isn't free.
Commitment to it is the fee.
Commitment though sometimes there's pain.
Commitment though sometimes there's rain.
Commitment to our chosen path.
Commitment without fear or wrath.
The knowledge that freedom comes with hate
from those who don't appreciate
true freedom helps us all be great,
once fear is not our chosen state.
Love the freedom. Love the choice;
to keep our peace and raise our voice.
Each moment gives us each the chance
to sing our songs and do our dance.
To live with gratitude and grace
through every up and down we face.

## CLIMBING SUN

I rise to meet the climbing sun
as it calls me out by name.
And challenges me to chase it down
to see from whence it came.
I chase it through dawn and midday
and almost into night.
But, of course, I lost it
when it sunk out of sight.
I rise to meet the climbing sun
while it lets me know who I am.
And calls to me to take small steps
To do the best I can.
I take the rising sun's advice
that steady wins the race.
Because the sun shares brilliant light
 I've found my natural place.
I rise to meet the climbing sun
to ride it across the sky.
To relish its warmth and absorb its light
and see how high I'll fly
I ride through it's slow decline
dismounting on the Earth
Tonight, I'll rest and prepare myself
for the sun's rebirth.

VICTORY SONG

Mountains fall and all else fails.
The lies we tell through colored tales
of better lives that we regale to hide the truth-
that horror hails-
of flames around the corner.
When ragged truths that we pursue
seem complex, although they're true,
no colored tales, just clearer hue
are openly explained to you.
Then you know you're a goner.
Still, those who rule through tales and lies
employing their nefarious spies,
and use of electronic eyes
on land and sea and in the skies
will give you what you want.
It's through unbridled death you find
the things they label right, unkind.
Where once advanced you fall behind,
finding those with opened eyes resigned,
to exorcise their haunts.
The seasoned vets all seem to know.
The uninitiated go.
Those in-between move to and fro,
while rulers govern and bestow
laws without consensus.
The end is nigh, and death is near
for all those who still exist here.
The lies dilute the truth, that's clear,
promote base feelings and stark fear
so, all raise their defenses.
But still, we live and still we fight.
We still venture into the night

and seek to reinforce what's right
so we can all walk in the light:
And be our higher selves.
Each moment, through the words we say,
committed to a brighter day.
Actions create and find the way.
Until we're there this firm foreplay
is as deep as we dare delve.
We fight to climb the mountain high;
the seas to conquer; the skies to fly;
to bolster truth o'er every lie;
to know the world beyond the eye-
Just to continue climbing.
We own our lives both right and wrong.
Each failed attempt just makes us strong.
And we can sing our victory song,
because our souls are shining.

## BIG DECISION

A natural conclusion. Unwanted delusion.
That's what has happened to me.
Unexpected confusion of a deceptive collusion
has suddenly set me free.
To be consciously flighty
and outrageously mighty
as I exercise the man I am.
Unrepentant and rightly
prouder than I might be
if things would turn out like I plan.
And though it may seem
that I'm thoughtless and mean,
it seems that's all that will work.
For when my thoughts are clean
the pickings are lean.
Success lies in being a jerk.
But what do I lose
if I walk in those shoes
and give up the man that is me?
Which man do I choose?
It's my soul I might bruise.
My soul I'll set completely free.
So, now as I write
on this now lonely night
I reflect on my latest revision.
Now I set my sight
on tomorrow's first light
in hopes of a brighter decision.

## MISSING THE TRAIN

Do you ever sit and listen
to the world
telling truths of nature?
Of spirit?
Of life?
How wondrous it is?
How loving it can be?
Where you fit?
Why "why" doesn't matter?
That being is greater than doing?
How much more it accomplishes?
Or are you so busy doing,
that the world passes you by?

## SILVER LINING

We all strive to find it.
That silver lining in each moment; in each breath.
We want it to be apparent.
To be revealed without walking the path.
Without training for life.
Without battling the dark.
Yet, it's never revealed until the deed is done.
The mountain climbed and the avalanche survived.
Limbs may be lost, or souls gone home,
belongings burned or crushed or lost.
And it still may not appear until years and tears have passed.
Or it may avail itself of your wisdom
and appear while the structure burns.
Still, the silver lining is just a sign,
an indicator that no matter how dark the morning,
a light will arise.
That despite the harshness and pain, there will come a soothing.
The silver lining is the chance to regroup, be thankful and grow,
to recognize the chance to be better
And walk the path some more.

## BIRD STORY

I've been missing the meat of the story.
I've looked over the obvious clues.
It's really not that complicated.
It requires that I change my views.
The bird eats its seed without worry
though the seed that is there's not enough.
The bird still returns to the feeder.
Sometimes it's just empty. Life's tough.
The filler leaves seed for the bird songs.
The birds sing their songs as they eat.
Then more birds flock to the feeder.
The filler, listening, takes a seat.
The bird eating seed doesn't worry.
At least there is seed to be had.
If the bird comes and the feeder is empty,
the bird just sings. It doesn't get mad.
Filler still gets to hear the bird song,
Although the bird doesn't have seeds to eat.
Wait too long and the bird will stop coming.
No bird and the bird song deletes.
From the meat of the story,
the needs of both sides must be met.
It states in this allegory,
if you don't give then you don't get.

## FEAR THE SKY

Once, when I was very young,
I saw a dragonfly.
Now that I'm a grown man,
somehow, I fear the sky.
Yes, it's a great blue expanse
the eye can't really see.
Nothing on Earth can or will touch it.
Especially not me.
It follows me where I go,
sometimes blanketed in clouds.
And sometimes on those darker days,
it doth protest too loud.
Flashing lights and roaring
it makes its presence known.
Sometimes with just a downpour,
sometimes frightening to the bone.
Usually though, the sky shines bright
and stays clear through the night.
The sun, the moon, the stars, I see,
calm me with their celestial light.
While I do still fear the sky
and to its power yield,
the lights that shine down day and night
provide a worthy shield.
So, I can go about my way
and keep on climbing high,
knowing I'm protected
with no need to fear the sky.

CHANCED DANCE
I broke the chains in Charlotte.
No one could hold me down.
Released what they called darkness.
My real voice came around.
Don't call me by my title.
Call me by my name.
Titles describe my standing
while I'm more like a flame
providing light in dark times.
Igniting kindling too.
Sparking consuming fires
and other things flames do.
I'll come up nice and quiet,
then roar onto the stage.
Make everybody chance their dance
regardless of their age.
Then when my time is over
and I chanced my last dance,
I'll leave the world silently
With one last sideways glance.

## OWNING OUR TIME

Creator of the universe,
every praise and every curse.
Every word in every verse.
God is in the Air.
$H_2O$ and skies of blue;
want to know what still holds true
in every faith and every hue?
God is everywhere.
Every who and everything.
Volcanoes and wedding rings.
Every pauper. Every king.
God includes them all.
Every planet. Every star.
Every quark and all quasars.
Out in space both near and far.
Creation does not stall.
Yet we try to run away
from the truth and how it plays.
And hope the lies of man can stay
as rules for how life goes.
But there are crimes against man's laws.
Without creation there are flaws.
And man won't admit he's the cause,
so the devil owns his woes.
Still, life is choice, action and being.
That's a truth there's no point fleeing.
To be something starts with us seeing
by virtue of our mind's eye.
Then what we want can be for real.
 Be something no one else can steal.
Accomplished purpose that we feel,
as we begin to fly.

Creations, then will light the path.
Make easy all the complex math.
Increase the fun delete the wrath,
so higher still we climb.
As we reach our highest peak
and see the answers that we seek,
we'll see that not a soul is weak
as we all own our time.

# DREAMS

I rise to see the Sandman leaving,
trailed by sleepy dust he throws.
The increased rhythm of my breathing
signals what the waking knows:
"Goodbye sleep and good by dreaming.
Hello world there's work to do".
Time for life and time for scheming.
Eating, growing, loving too.
Yes, I'll miss that world of wonder.
In some ways the nightmares too.
Although they tear my world asunder,
waking makes them all untrue.
Now it's time to make the real ones
and learn from real nightmares' fear.
Like dreams, looking back seems fun,
but nightmares persist with backward stares.
Awake, it's time to move life forward.
Awake, it's time to meet our goals.
Our dreams are what we're moving towards.
Our dreams are what will make us whole.
So, leave the nightmares far behind you
and let their lessons make us great.
Achieve our goals; our dreams will come true.
If we don't move, our dreams don't wait.
When next the leaving sandman finds you,
be too damn tired for sleeping dreams.
Be close enough to your real goals
to know what "life is a dream" means.

## LEAPING DOG

I watch my dog chase squirrels in trees forty feel high.
Despite the height of this leaping,
he can never touch the sky.
Nor can he climb the trees where they chitter, chatter, squeal.
Yet, he continues leaping
as though the space to them is not real.
I believe he keeps on trying because he believes he's free
to defy the laws of physics
and get up in that tree.
I see it as a metaphor
to achieve, in life, success.
You won't know if you'll make it
if you give up on the test.
You won't know if it's possible
to have your dream come true,
if you don't give all your effort
to see the journey through.
Now, I'm sure my dog will leap on
until he can leap no more
or until he spots a bushed squirrel
and knocks it to the forest floor.
Once he has his goal in tow,
he'll lay down satisfied
and like us he will celebrate
the fact he always tried.

EMBRACE

It's out there; and we keep our eyes closed
as we fly by the seat of our pants.
We create pains to cry about
while tightening our circle for living.
We damn the free opinion;
shackle freedom's dissent.
Seeking a world of comfort
when life shows it never exists for long.
From the beginning of time
change has been constant.
Ignorantly, we fight to hold it still.
Reluctant to recognize that the embrace
can only bring us peace;
will surely build our strength;
improves grit and resilience;
and generates a smile.
For when the next transition arrives
we will be smarter; better; stronger;
knowing we'll know more
each time we'll be tested.
Distress will ease with
the conclusion revealing peace.
Embrace change. Embrace growth.
Embrace grit. Embrace love.
Embrace!

## FRUIT TREES

There's a million ways to get to man or woman from a child.
A million small experiences to make them mild or wild.
A thousand tiny focuses to make them great or small.
Far too many instances to focus on them all.
What we really get to do is stand tall, proud and free.
Then make sure in their daily lives that we're the ones they see.
Give them the chance to recognize it's awesome to be smart.
Don't judge the folks who seem slow, just recognize their heart.
Explain all have their talents. None of them show the same.
Ours may be called intelligence, theirs called by another name.
Dictate that we all should love ourselves, our talents and our flaws.
And recognize our shortcomings are talents in the raw.
Judge not others lest ye be judged. Our life's all we control.
Don't demand outcomes of others; each life plays its own role.
Other peoples' business will not complete your plan.
It will provide you enemies to combat where you stand.
Learn to live with empathy and exercise your grace.
For nothing greater makes this world a more livable life space.
Remember that the children are the future of our tree.
So how we fertilize decides how strong it will be.
Will it bear fruit next season? And will that fruit be sweet?
Or will that fruit, dead on the vine, lay rotting at our feet?
Let's hold young people higher. Let's give them what they need.
Let's keep their souls inspired to work hard to succeed.
Whatever that might mean to them, let's help them find their way.
So, they may raise their own fruit trees successfully one day.

## BATTLE WORN

Battle worn and living weary,
I combat demons in my mind,
though their voices often scare me,
playing havoc with my time.
Thus, long gone but not forgotten,
beautiful dreams on pyres lay.
Undone by fear and doubt so rotten,
thus the demons' fires play.
So, here I sit my dreams now ashes,
the pyre out, my path denied.
No way to have what I thought promised.
Again, I feel my mentors lied.
Hold! I have found a slight forgiveness
with slight possibility.
A small chance that I might win this battle
to let my oppressed soul free.
If I love myself a little,
then that love for me will grow.
My faith in myself will grow too,
until dreams come true is all I'll know.
It's not the goal that really counts, though.
It's what I learn along the way.
One goal ends, the next begins
so the knowledge gained will always stay.
So, battle worn and living weary,
those demons seem to leave me now.
Persistent they still hang out near me.
Accepting them, this I allow.
As my shaken mind gets better,
accepting all I am inside,
my soul becomes my sole protector
and by God's grace I will abide.

## LET ME

Let me try the world escaping. Let me try this life to flee.

I can see myself evading all the trouble chasing me.

Let me sing my lamentations; sing in song my wretched pain.

Let me show it off in stages; violence from which I refrain.

Angry, I have blessed answers and with fear my love display.

Carefully I take big chances to be happy when I play.

My full growth I cannot yet show; thoughts too high for folks to see,

simplified in ways that I know. Still, the world just won't let me

TRUTH NOW

As we flow through life.
A ripple in time.
We change the flow of history.
But not history itself.
Only knowing now.
We knowingly, or unknowingly,
write our stories
without knowing how they'll read.
When they are read.
In the end, though,
it will seem purposeful.
For the lessons learned
and answers gained
will fuel our journey to enlightenment
and, looking back,
light our path to our current truth.

## UNMOVING FAITH

It seems I'm highly favored. I simply must know why.
What keeps me in the eye of that we call "most high"?
How does it come to pass that I'm considered so?
That God would have my back almost everywhere I go?
Maybe I'm blessed because God's praises I sing.
Or it's just because being there is God's thing.
I hope I feel this way and can maintain God's grace
when with tragedy God chooses to, this joy, replace.
I hope that I'll remember then that God has me in the plan
of the storied tale that's put in place for man.
I hope I can still stand tall and hold my head up high
with knowledge that in time God will let the sad go by.
I trust I'll remember well that God is in it all.
If I have unmoving faith, God won't let me fall.

VALUE OF PRIVACY
What is the value of privacy?
It keeps our secrets ours. It lets us play our lurid little games
amongst our fenced yard flowers.
What is the value of privacy?
It keeps us feeling safe from prosecutions, insults, and barbs
against how we live in this space.
What is the value of privacy?
In our space we are great. While judgment looms outside of here,
in our space we are great.
What is the value of privacy?
My riches I can hide. So, those who stand watch constantly
can't take away my pride.
What is the value of privacy?
We record all we do. Computers, cell phones, databases.
Is privacy true?
What is the value of privacy?
All the secrets it creates? No matter how you live your life
there's distrust outside the gates.
What is the value of privacy
that governments promote? The secrets that they hold from us
has got us by the throats.
What is the value of privacy?
In the wrong hands it leads to war
and keeps the populace confused
about what they're fighting for.
What is the value of privacy?
It keeps us all apart when all the things we try to hide,
we all did at the start.
What is the value of privacy
When we are all the same? When I am cut, do I not bleed?
I'm tired of playing this game.

RIVERVIEW

A life without direction is a life on open seas,
where the only direction is the direction of the breeze.
That's not to say that you won't end up high and dry.
But the storms you'll have to go through are hardly worth the try.
It's better that a course is set; like on a river wide-
instead of on the ocean vast relying on the tide.
The river has a starting point and, also, has an end.
So, you'll know where you'll finish and where your path began.
A river is banked on either side. You can rest along the way.
Rejuvenate your heart and mind at learning or at play.
The banks provide parameters to keep you tried and true.
So, you don't stray afar or wide.
You stay aligned the whole way through.
Choose a goal and make a plan. Stick to it until the end.
Commit to where you're going, even when the river bends.
And when you finally get there, you'll look back and see it's true.
That journey on the river provided the greatest view.

## AZURE GUIDE

I stare in the light of a cobalt sky, as dreams fly to my heart,
amazed at their boldness of clarity and strength.
I am forced to consider the honor of receiving such sights.
Bestowed with the responsibility of creating truth from an idea.
A voice reasons I am the right one, though wrong to others I seem,
while the heavens bellow my name exposing the path I must walk.
Lighting the trail while people build arrows
 to clear the obstacles before me.
Like the earth by the sun. The trees by the rain.
I am blessed.
I stare in the light of an indigo sky,
and follow the path to destiny's calling.

## BROKEN LIFE

Patterns of a broken life
lay damaged in the snow
and all I can do is stare.
No blood. No bones.
Just crystallized tears
and screams frozen in place.
Destiny turned in on itself
as if a wall or a sudden gale
had forced it from its path.
But I've no time to stand and stare.
My journey's still to be completed.
So, I move on remembering
patterns of a broken life
and commit to not
making them mine.

## SEEING DREAMS

I sit in a dream world, where all I dream is real.
Of all the things I dream about, what's real is what I feel.
I let the dream things rule me, as though they all are true.
I let their gaze offend me each day my whole life through.
But then my eyes were opened to things I can achieve.
The things that I can become, if only I believe.
The knowledge I'll acquire if I let my mind be still.
The success I'll inspire, if I exercise the will.
Now my dreams are just that. Asleep and when awake.
Decided by my own will with every step I take.
I make my own beginnings. My ends I clearly see.
Completely I believe that the things I see I 'll be

## FIGHTING FOR BALANCE

The sails don't fail when the wind doesn't blow.
Unless anchored, the boat won't stand still.
Such is the way of things that even if the eye can't see,
movement is constant.
So too is change.
On the brightest, calmest, most glorious day,
the darkest, most tempestuous, atrocious day
waits in the wings.
This, not to spoil the greatness, but to exalt it.
To lift it higher when it is gone,
than it is perceived when it is present.
Just as the great day waits in the wings, when darkness
presents boldly in the moment,
to provide reprieve and peace, revealing the lessons learned.
Darkness will teach without allowing learning.
Light will allow learning without providing lessons.
They are two sides of the same coin.
As spring won't pause to let summer in,
light, nor dark, will pause for the other.
They circle each other, fighting for balance.

## THE SCARS

We are not in a space where we can bear our scars proudly.
If we did so, others might protest loudly.
We won't even accept them for ourselves,
thus, creating dark places where our psychology dwells.
If we accept them, there's a chance our psychology heals.
Then we can change the way our psyche feels.
Learn to accept the scars that others bear.
Show them the way, and how much we care.
We all get hurt and we all form scars.
We're all sometimes ignorant of how lucky we are.
A scar means we've lived for another day's fight.
That we get to heal. The next time, get it right.
A scar makes us stronger and smarter still.
It provides us with more knowledge to bend life to our will.
If we accept our scars and those of others at least,
maybe we can create a world filled with love and peace.

## NOT IN THE FACE

Not in the face! Please... Don't strike me there.
You wouldn't cause such pain. Not if you care.
Keep telling me lies so I don't get hurt.
I'll give you anything. From my back, my shirt.
I don't need the truth if it will torture me.
Leave me to believe I'm totally free.
Leave me alone. Let me realize.
I guess in my own time I'll open my eyes.
I'll choose my comfort and my own pace.
Strike how you like, but not in the face.
You say you'll leave me and go your own way?
With someone who won't see, you just cannot stay?
You say that you're growing and taking shots well?
Hey, not in the face! That just sounds like hell.
I'll hold onto my comfort and grow when it's time.
Life's good for me right now while I'm in my prime.
I may not be growing as fast as I could
or moving forward like an adult should.
The way I see it, this life's not a race.
Don't push me. Don't rush me, and not in the face.
You say you won't lie. You'll tell me the truth.
Well, I'm always going to ask you for proof.
It's not that I don't trust you. I'm not ready for change.
And I know that my choices might leave us estranged.
So, if you must go, I guess I'll adapt.
You'll be free of me and won't feel entrapped.
Look, I can't control life and my feeling's legit.
Though you cry "excuses", well you're full of shit.
So, leave me alone to stand in this place.
Love may show in my heart, but not in the face.
I stand here alone in the departure lounge
feeling sorry for the way all this bullshit went down.

You shouting expletives, me trying to stay calm.
Just trying to stop others from raising alarms.
I accept I upset you with my stubborn ways.
Yet, I still respect you despite how this plays.
My feelings, alone here, are not hard to trace.
This break-up strikes hard, but not in the face.

## GR(IT)

Tomorrow's Friday left me here.
Alone with no one around to care.
On all sides bound by abject fear.
No courage left to fight it.
The day after, I took a knee.
I closed my eyes, so I won't flee
Then, prayed for God to rescue me-
from sorrow laden shit.
I rose, after, to stand so tall
that all my problems seemed quite small.
Emboldened by God's mystic call,
my soul was, now, full lit.
I walked the walk I used to talk.
Vowed nothing else would make me balk.
Only solutions, I now stalk.
Just knowing I won't quit.
Four days from Sunday, I am fine.
Tomorrow's Friday. Life's sublime.
My spirit, now, I can't confine.
There's not a place it fits.

## UNTIL DEATH

Smoke 'em if you got 'em. Roll them all the way.
Today will end tomorrow. This moment will not stay.
Sun drops beneath the horizon. The night sky will not last.
Then, before you know it, right now becomes the past.
So, shine while the fire's burning. Blind us at every turn.
With talent, guts, and knowledge, show us how bright you burn.
Fly higher than earth's ceiling and farther than its sun.
Run longer than you ever have, until your dreams are done.
The present is a gift, they say, that lasts all of one breath.
So many stacked together is living ... until your death.

## THE SPIRIT'S CROWN

I walk where most men fear to crawl.
I soar where most won't fly.
With strange bravado through it all,
since I know that I won't die.
I see beyond the ocean's edge,
where once sail ships would fall.
I stand upon cliff face's ledge,
in hopes I'll appear tall.
My real hope?  To see heaven's gates
while life flows through these veins.
Don't worry, I'll run while death waits
and prayer stalls hell's cold flames.
I want to live a good long life
while helping others rise.
Gain knowledge from the sacrifice
turning others lows to highs.
I plan to be a happy man;
walk life's path with a smile.
Yet, I'll accomplish all I can,
each foot, each yard, each mile.
Then, when at last I am laid down,
I'll know I've done it all.
That's when I'll don the spirit's crown.
I'll answer the final call.

PLACES I'VE BEEN

Today I'm not the man I was when I left my home.
I'm the sullied product of the places I have roamed.
Those places that hold pieces of what was naivete.
Where I explored and I did work, and I often played.
I left my home with many rules; with a set state of mind.
Consorted with no one not following my beliefs in kind.
But varied adventures required different trains of thought.
I realized the lost time that my ignorance had wrought.
Today, I keep an open mind, my story isn't yours.
We may spend time in the same place and still have different tours.
I can't judge the world by what's seen through your eyes.
Things seen through mine create completely different ties.
Still, I have faith today, that the places I have seen
are not the same places today as the places I have been.
That what naivete then labeled awesome and quite grand,
today may seem mundane; poorly thought out where they stand.
My eyes are opened wider to things that they discern.
Not everything that scares me, do I want to burn.
I'm open to what's offered as opportunity to grow,
To leave behind the home I left, for a new one that I know.

## STATEMENTS MOVING

What does rolling forward mean from a position standing still?
Is it even possible?
A state of motion that creates a change in scenery?
A frightening condition that leaves the familiar behind?
A sacrifice of comfort for the hope of better?
Is it realizing potential?
Is it testing a theory?
Is it diving into the depths and darkness of the unknown
with no confirmation of where you'll stop?
Is it even worth it?
We could stand still. Await the passing of time and tide.
Watch the scenery change around us like seasons.
Play it safe. Hold onto what we've got.
Know that tomorrow brings the same outcome.
Hope that it does, anyway.
Hold onto our potential.
Take no chance on just a theory.
Be safe in the light of the known.
We may not get better, and it might not get worse.
Instead of rolling forward, we can hold the line.
But should we die with regret, or satisfaction?

## ONE MORE BREATH

Every day we fight the war:
Good and evil; right and wrong; yes and no.
We decide. We judge, even if only ourselves.
We mark our success with smiles.
Our failures in memories to be released at a later time.
We try to cling to the laughs that fade with repetition.
We bury the hurts that shine with the unexpected.
All this, while living and loving. Going and growing.
Marching towards the inexorable conclusion
that is our foregone demise.
Yet rarely do we try to do things differently.
The toys and tools change.
The values conflate reality.
We hold onto old wounds.
Some, experienced by ancestors long dead,
and fight for the right to be seen.
Only to be heard by folks readying for their own battles.
In the end, we regret the battles.
We are saddened by the combat.
We wish we loved and played more.
And those values we conformed to?
Well, they are nothing compared to one more breath.

## SEASONS IN WORDS

Every now and then the rain comes down
to soak the grounds I roam.
To awaken the green from winter's cold
and beautify my home.
Not that there's no beauty in winter.
For then the sun shines its purest light.
The bare bones of trees permitting the moon
to brighten the ground through the night.
It's like life as we live it
when upheaval seems to block our way.
It's not as though we get nothing from it
and bad times never come to stay.
Even when life is at its darkest,
there still emerge times we can laugh.
These are the times we can gather our strength
and sometimes cut the dark times in half.
So, life is just like the four seasons,
or two if you live way down south.
Whether snow or rain, plants die, grow again,
and life changes like words from our mouth.

## SOMEWHERE IN THE DARK

Somewhere in the dark is the light.
Floating brightly. Welcoming every soul.
Challenging the search is the dark.
Awaiting its discovery is the light.
As I stare in the mirror,
my greatest obstacle stares back.
The dark floats in my eyes.
Fear, welling in my belly.
Courage sparking, not burning, in my heart.
My soul screaming to light the way.
Somewhere in the dark is the light.
I will trudge through the least of these
in hopes to near the solace of enlightenment.
Desiring to see the glow.
Hoping there is warmth.
Believing I'll find my home.
Praying the light will have me:
And I won't remain in the dark.

## NOW IS THE TIME

Now is the time to love your life.
Now is the time that matters.
Now is the time to raise the glass
and enjoy the sound if it shatters.
Yesterday has come and gone
making all it holds the past.
Unchanging. Unmoving. Unfettered
with its results firmly cast.
The future can only be seen;
visions now that may never come.
It's literally a waking dream;
a circumstance we haven't yet won.
Now is the time to get your happiness.
Now is the time to make your start.
Now is the time to feel your joy;
make the bread, turn the soil, form the art.
Yes, you can foresee the future.
You'll never end up living there.
Memories of the past may haunt you.
Remember that the past doesn't care.
Now is when all things exist.
Before, they didn't, nor down the road.
The past and future are just burdens.
The present is what bears the load.
Before you give up on the current,
remember past and future change.
Research, feelings, and weak memories;
all make new old memories strange.
Here and now all things exist.
The present is where we can and do.
Work within the now you're given.
Make your current life anew.

## TRUTH AND LIES

Given that words communicate, and action demonstrates,
Truth, then, lies in the eyes and not the ears.
Speaking and writing let you know
circumstances and maybe so's
while experience knows your true joys and fears.
Words reveal the pathways to excitement in life.
Action gives the heart something to hold.
Words manipulate the world actions tend to reveal.
Thus, truth is bought while lies are always sold.

## FORTITUDE IN ANGUISH

Anguish drives the guilty heart, and also stirs the soul.
It disrupts the innocent mind when anguish comes to call.
Anguish builds its own truths from past and present times.
It contorts displayed proof, to suit its new design.
Relationships are compromised; tested from head to feet.
When anguish steps into the room, it's always with a wreath.
While foundations being strong in minds
that know and love their strength
may mean the wreath does not get lain
but stretched to its full length.
Still, anguish remains hard to defeat, although its source may fade.
Even with one's spirits high, anguish we can't evade.
Anguish urges us to push through or surrender on the spot.
It distinguishes those with fortitude from those who have it not.

## LEGACY

One thinks they must leave a legacy.
Well then, live a good life.
Leave an example to follow.
Find a goal and see it through.
Love yourself more than you love others,
but be kind to others more than you are to yourself.
When you look in the mirror, be tough love.
When you turn from the mirror, be tough love.
Remember words can't hurt you, regardless how they sting.
They may be delivered with venom, but they can be the antidote.
How they are received by you is your choice.
Change is constant: inside and outside you.
You can only adjust and adapt to outside change.
How you change internally is completely your choice.
View every event as a neutral occurrence
open to the interpretation of the experiencer.
That being said, your intention does not mean the outcome
will be viewed or received in the manner you seek.
For every action, there is an equal and opposite reaction.
These are called consequences, even if emotions are involved.
Your legacy may not be what you intended.
The living make the rules. The dead rest in peace.

## PAST LIVES LIVED

What if I ran through the woods, littered with the memories
of past lives lived?
Will I remember the ones that brought me pain?
The days when laughter was my only food?
The nights when love walked through the door;
only to leave me crying once I knew it was gone?
Will those memories, strewn like decaying leaves
on rain moistened soil, disintegrate like snow in spring?
Or come back to life with April's rain.
Can my joy return to me like that of a child surrounded by friends
in a playground: effortless? Effervescent? Free?
Or will the shadow of fear; the weight of pride;
the weakness of ego continues to keep me here?
Unable to run through a wood littered with the memories
of past lives lived.

## ANSWERS

I was born to question living.
Its ins and outs. Its ups and downs.
Most importantly, its whys.
Confined to the limitations of human skin,
I've questioned more than answers can afford.
Still, I continue to ask, committed to search.
Yet, answers abound.
They are in the lives whose truths we can't understand.
They're in the eyes of children we ignore.
Answers live in the people we serve.
The ones whose pain we take on; whose lacking we relieve.
Those whose empty space we fill with kindness.
I begin to find that the more questions I ask,
the brighter my purpose becomes.
I am consumed by it.
So much so, my questions are answered
by deeds.

## FEEL BLESSED

I never don't feel blessed.
Even when things aren't their best.
I never don't feel blessed.
I never feel I'm cast aside.
When I'm confused and low on pride.
When I've lost my way or skipped my stride.
When I feel, to me, the whole world has lied.
I never feel I'm cast aside.
I never feel I'm truly lost.
Not even when my world is tossed.
When others, over my words, gloss.
When they deny what my time costs.
I never feel I'm truly lost.
I always feel a light within.
During times when things look dim.
During those times when I may sin.
Definitely when I'm with my kin.
For the wrongs that I rescind.
I always feel a light within.
I truly never don't feel blessed.
Whether I'm serious or I jest.
Whether I pass or fail the test.
I truly never don't feel blessed.

## A LIFE OF BOLD RETURN

Live a life of bold return
and give beyond compare.
Live in hopes you can release us
from this cruddy shit we share.
Live to provide love
and bolster self-respect.
To recognize one's status
and their talents detect.
Live to see the brightness of their skills
and read between the lines.
Put to creative uses
their intelligent young minds.
Promote "respect each other".
Your story is all your own.
"Be proud of who you really are
from the skin down to the bone."
Don't bend to their oppressive will.
Rise up and grab your star.
Ignore jibes and racist taunts.
Show the world who you are.
We come from the founders of the world.
Builders of science and math.
Travelers to places near and far.
It's us who laid the path.
We never sought to conquer.
We're not here to oppress.
In fact, it's in our DNA
to share and uplift the rest.
So, recognize now who you are.
The power that's inside.
Love yourself for what you are.
For those like you have pride.

Bring no harm to others.
Instead show them the way.
Help make this world a better place
where all of us can play.

## POWER WE HAVE WITHIN

The goal is to not die being still;
to not perish like a beached whale- covered at high tide.
We are the creators of civilization.
The builder of worlds. The tamers of fire.
It is we that first explored beyond our borders.
Who collected knowledge. Who shared knowledge.
Who recognized the creator of all things in everything around us.
It is we who saw it in ourselves.
We are blessed to be where we are.
It should drive us to stand tall.
It should help us re-identify our values.
It should motivate us to once again
exercise that power we have within.
Yes. There are physical and spiritual powers against us.
Yes. We are oppressed from a certain point of view.
Yes. The current system seeks to deny us
even as it seeks to reinforce our resolve;
to reenergize our spirit
and reawaken the desire to be greater than our circumstances.
The goal is to die on our feet. To dance to the music of this life.
To run full speed to the next adventure
completely exhausting the power we have within.
Death should find us walking slowly, pondering events to come.
Surprising us that growth is done
until we materialize as matter again.

## NIGHT CAPTURED

Captured by the night, born long after the sun is down.
Rising on the ashes of a day burnt sky.
I look on the horizon of a growing eve
to find the truth of my existence. A why.
Wandering a myriad of roads lain down
by the builders who ventured before.
I learn as I grow and watch the stars
where my enlightened truth should soar.
But along the route I'm shackled
by a fear that I can't deny.
I'm forced to fight feelings I have,
if I ever want to fly.
I'm forced to forge a new lane;
create my own philosophy.
If I ever want to realize my dreams
And metamorphosize to a truer me.
I rise above the laid paths, look deeper into night.
My lane leads deeper into the dark if I want to see my light.
I wade into the darkness as I build a newer path.
I drop bits of crumbs upon it that consist of my old math.
The pathway becomes easier the bolder I become.
I think I am beginning to see the dawn of a rising sun.

## BLUE SKY

Different shades of O2 or N2 light the sky.
From the moment the sun rises to six hours past its high.
Those shades promote a feeling artists represent in hues
that range from sullen sadness to playful loving cues.
Of course, sometimes gray jumps in. So too, sometimes, does red.
The greys with gloom or thunder, the other vibrant dread.
Portents of rain and dark days or volcanoes wicked glow.
Fire in the distance, red hues horizons show.
Still, blue looks down upon it, that azure firmament,
aware, despite occurrence, blue sky will not relent.

LIFE'S PHILOSOPHY
"Why are we here?" is the question
when all that is, just is.
When everything is just one thing
and as part of this thing we live.
"Well then, what makes our lives have meaning?"
Just being is meaning enough.
We should be aware of our sameness.
Belief we're apart makes life tough.
"Well, why must we suffer with dying?"
A transition from being apart.
A chance to perceive our won greatness.
A chance to believe there's a start.
A chance to believe that creation began
with a word and a bang.
A chance to put time on an essence
in whose space life constantly sang.
"So, why should I bother with living
if in reality I'm always here?"
Because life is a place of constant change
and here you have options to care.
Life provides chances to create.
Life provides chances to fear.
Life provides chances to love and doubt.
Life provides chances to share.
Life provides chances to see ourselves
and our souls in each other's eyes.
Life provides chances to honor ourselves;
to witness our infinite size.

## THE OLD MAN

Every man thrives in an environment of his comfort;
a world, the depths of which, he understands.
In which he feels at home.
Outside of that looms chaos.
A disturbed state that creates unease.
Yet, even to this, every man can adjust:
But loses his way back to the world known before.
Birds of adaptation feed on the crumbs of change.
The return trip is harder than first being there.
The old man may never be found again.

DEAR FATHER

The 'W' rose above anything he'd had in mind.

The fact the first born was a male had proved the world most kind.

The 'I' was for initiative. Integrity. Insight.

Creative to extricate from almost any plight.

The 'S' was meant for subtlety and also meant for smart.

Sensitive. Successful and sharp would play a part.

'E', the end. The family. The ancestors and more.

A means to honor all of those who rose and died before.

Dear Father:

I write to express my love for you; resentment and disdain for you
I could not share before.

I'll never understand you- at least not to your core.

I accept the man you used to be. The one that you became.

I respect the first man who gave me my current name.

There are days I miss you, though you left so long ago.

I reminisce about the times your love and humor showed.

But there were tears and pain too, in those days so distant past.

I thank God for change and growth that will not let bad times last.

I climb a figurative tree of life, so I am heaven bound.

One day I will wake up in the place where your soul's found.

There we'll laugh over a drink- ambrosia or some wine-

about how all life's challenges always end up fine.

We'll reflect on how what's meant to be helps make us who we are;
although through all life's changes, we never venture far.

Far from who we think we are or who we want to be.

Far from all the childhood dreams of the grown-up life we'd see.

We'll talk about our life plans; the results that realized.

Identify the areas where we both compromised.

Identify the shortcomings and growth we must address
the next time we are so blessed to together manifest.

As I confess my love for you through all our trials and strain,
and let you know that through it all, I'd do it all again.

## MOMENTS GONE

Exemplify the newness of moments from the last.
Worry not about the moments that have already passed.
The new ones allow growth every single day.
The old ones you can't change no matter what folks say.
Even if you could, is that what you would do?
Lessons learned yesterday allow for plans anew.
Mistakes are simply tries, that aren't perfect yet.
So, if you try again, then perfect you might get.
At least one step closer to your chosen goal
One step closer to feeling completely whole.
Even if you don't, the journey can be great.
Fall down, get up and try again. You'll always challenge fate.
So, let your moments passed remain as that moment's gone.
Put to use your lessons and your journey won't be long.
Keep a present mind: A 'be here now' mindset.
Open the door you've trained for; the dream you want you'll get.

## THE THRONE ROOM

I believe I've mastered the throne room.
Its size. Its depth. Its space.
For when I enter the throne room,
it becomes a divine place.
It's quiet, serene, in the throne room.
A great place to let loose my mind,
and, if no one else shares the throne room,
a nice place to read. I find.
There are general rules for the throne room.
Though we each get to set our own.
The air is kept clean in the throne room.
No one should leave soiled, the throne.
The rules that I've set for the throne room:
No food; no drink; no noise.
Seats down for the ladies in the throne room.
Clean up after standing, boys.
Let's all raise our cups to the throne room.
We'll drink then we'll piss it out.
It's trees and soft leaves with no throne room.
The john's what this one's about.

HAIL!
Hail! To the enlightened and their love of the present,
that past lives and future forfend.
The enlightened and wise keep open their eyes
while the rest change the past, well, pretend.
Hail! To the change that forever remains
but can only be viewed in the past.
Though it's happening now, right here beneath our brow,
with change this new moment won't last.
Hail! To the living: That's all of us here
who can't know what the future will hold.
There, change and age and potential are staged,
and for all here our death is foretold.
Hail! To the dead who prepared our stead,
who lived lives that were harder than ours.
Who cried not for a name or fortune or fame
and stood proud, though now pushing up flowers.
Hail! To the loved and the ones that now love.
May they consume the people who hate.
Dissolve the fear that hangs here and there
before we find it's too late.
Hail! To the God involved in it all.
May all things wake up to its name.
To honor its might and live in its light
and forever in its love remain.
Hail! Hail! HAIL!

## IN THE ABYSS

Still, the light's beyond me a tunnel's length away.
I walk forward with an internal drive to see the light of day.
Though I'll no longer be trudging through this muck,
feeling my way along dank, moist walls,
I know that stepping into the light means I will be seen
by others who desire to see me in the abyss.
This challenge I must not fear, for it is in the abyss
that I gained strength.
It is in the abyss that found courage.
It is in the abyss that I became wise.
In that stygian darkness that faith guided my steps,
holding my hand until the respite of the light.

## WHAT IT TAKES

Only one time to see the world the way I see it now.
Only one time to love the woman who loved me back somehow.
Only one time to live a life of fulfilled childhood dreams.
Only one time to lose a chance. Sometimes that's how it seems.
Only one time to make the choice to do what's right, not wrong.
Only one time to follow the crowd or choose to walk alone.
Only one time to take the time to correct the mistakes.
Only one time, one moment, that's just want it takes.
Only one time to love yourself like others and your things.
Only one time to praise yourself and feel the joy it brings.
Only one time to walk straight through the doors of the unknown.
Only one time to realize you won't walk through alone.

## THERE YOU ARE

Beyond wits end there is madness:
A cacophony of lights;
A vision of abject sadness,
and confusion of wrongs and rights.
That's where I sit with my feelings
as I watch the world implode
while man goes through his feigned dealings
while a dark bill of goods are sold.
So, now I find myself wanting
to return to my simpler days
when life didn't seem so daunting.
When men seemed to have simpler ways.
But alas, there's no use in malingering
just to reminisce on days in the past.
For that is the same as me fingering a snowflake.
Its form just won't last.
So, I must return to the present,
as my work has brought me this far.
Now is the season of my contentment.
I know wherever you go, there you are.

## FURTHER FROM CENTER

Spread ever thinner by the passage of time,
I constantly seek my center.
Seeing it from here, it is a light,
magnitudes above the brightest star,
and metaphorically just as far.
For I have wandered further from it than I ever imagined
my elliptical path would take me.
I float out here in a region of confusion that fights to inoculate me
Against thought of peace, love and togetherness.
But when I look to center, I can see the truth.
There lies calmness in the storms.
There lies peace in the battle.
There lies love, to combat fear.
There lies a longing for togetherness with other centered beings,
and the introduction of a new world where centered is the norm
and seeking center is being centered.

## THE FIRST CIRCLE

I sat in the first circle, and looking around, only saw me.
The expression on each face reflected all the ways I'd be.
I rose to stand above them. Yes, I stood proud and tall.
I told them I would love them, respect and accept them all.
We broke form the first circle and spread across the world.
I failed to recognize them when sticks and stones they hurled.
I'd lost the sense of circle and filled that space with fear,
although the next one in that circle stood next to me. Right here!
I searched through the world's libraries to prove the circle true.
I could no longer see it from my blinded point of view.
Now death stands before me with a face that looks like mine.
I'm beginning to realize; I was in the circle the whole time.
I sit in the first circle. The universe and me.
The deeper that I look within, the more of me I see.

## A CONFLUENCE OF "WHYS?"

We live our lives in the answer that is you
mapping our forgotten way to paradise,
unaware that the answer to the mystery of here
lies only behind closed eyelids and open hearts.
We pretend not to see our greatness,
complicating our lives with a confluence of whys,
when "it is what it is" will do.
We strive to be better than one another,
when no other than ourselves can we really supplant.
We do not recognize we are fish in a bowl
trying to see through the glass.
Mice in a maze trying to see the room.
Meanwhile, you are the architect and builder of structure
that our minds can't begin to grasp.
Yet, we try to see your plan and figure out your path
until our last breath when, maybe,
we get to ask you ourselves.

SEEKING INNOCENCE

During our yesterday, our naivete danced
linguistically around the facts of life.
We'd yet to understand,
craving absolution from ignorance.
We let our egos wield our shields
while our perspectives parried facts,
we'd yet to understand.
Wounded, we stood strong.,
shedding tears alone in dark corners.
Still smiling in the light.
Now, we long for such days.
Hardened by the truths of life,
we miss days of innocence
when we could be cut by small indiscretions,
wounded by wrong intonations.
When we lived mostly unguarded,
and able to enjoy to the fullest,
every experience of life.
We long to live free of the burdens
the shields of age have produced.
Innocence is only restored
In the moments we ignore the past
and pretend the future never comes.

# *Acknowledgement*

First and foremost, I must acknowledge the creator for allowing me to live this life and providing me with the courage to share this gift. I also want to acknowledge my family for their support in everything I've done and my friends for their guidance whenever I needed it. I want to give thanks and appreciation for the finest fighting force in the world and the great comrades I am honored to know from that experience: the United States Marine Corps. Semper Fi, Devil Dogs! Lastly, I want to thank those people in my life who have provided me a living example of how to succeed in realizing your dream. This book was one of mine. Thank you.

www.ingramcontent.com/pod-product-compliance
Ingram Content Group UK Ltd.
Pitfield, Milton Keynes, MK11 3LW, UK
UKHW041317240125
4283UKWH00035B/348